for Vladimir, Lilia, Konstantin, Tomy and Kosta

Acknowledgements:

Gregory O'Donoghue would like to thank Kristin
Dimitrova for her assistance in the translation of this book.

Cover image: *Shadow of Autumn* by Dimo Kolibarov etching
and aquatint 59cm x 65cm.

A Visit to The Clockmaker

Kristin Dimitrova

translated from the Bulgarian by
Gregory O'Donoghue

SOUTHWORD editions

First published in 2005
by Southword Editions,
the Munster Literature Centre,
Frank O'Connor House, 84 Douglas Street,
Cork, Ireland.

Set in Centaur
Printed in Ireland by Colour Books, Dublin.

ISBN: I-905002-03-3
www.munsterlit.ie

This book is the first in a series of thirteen published as
part of the official programme for Cork 2005: European
Capital of Culture

Contents

Searching for an Answer

I asked the sky
"Why am I here?"
It swallowed
my words & waited for more.

I wondered
what else I could add.

I asked the earth
"Why am I here?"
It shrugged its mountains.

I asked the fire
"Why am I here?"
Busily crackling
it did not hear a word.

I went to the well
& asked the water
"Why am I here?"
— "Come down to me
& I will tell you."

"Actually" I said
"I was only asking."

"The Messenger does not Matter"

Three hooded men have long
been walking the clouds
asking about you.

But you know, of course.

You breed pet moths in your room
& move chessmen, waiting for an answer.

It comes late, with your voice.

"Is that my voice?"

Yes, your own voice

  now,
  under the dying candlelight
  you will jump faster & faster.

"I'd rather not."

Oh, really!

Lie down
get up
lie down
get up
& copy life
in soft letters.

Noah, the Carrier

Noah told it differently.

To the Jewish delegation he said
after the raven he had sent out a dove —
Lo! she returned with an olive leaf.

*The dove is the white herald of joy, pure soul of the innocent
foretokening new life.*

The founding fathers approved the tale
& included it.

To Gilgamesh, however, he put it like this:

I sent out a dove but she came back.
I sent out a swallow, she also returned.
Finally, I sent a raven:
never saw him again —
then I knew he had found
dry land & prey.

*The raven is the black warrior among birds, a circling cut
in the good sky, first witness of the last transformation.*

This was the language of Gilgamesh.

Left to himself,
Noah murmured

"Truth does not
make a good myth
yet only myth can carry it."

He could clearly remember
it was the flies
that discovered the ark.

The Border

My daughter asked me whether
I had brought her bubble gum.

I told her I had not,
but I was there.

She objected that I was one thing
& bubble gum quite another.

I pointed out she could not always
expect something nice.

She corrected me
"Not something nice but bubble gum."

Although the sun was doing its best
& the birds interrupted each other

& the grass in the park was greedy-green,
my daughter rained her heart out.

There is a happy world & a sad one
& bubble gum in-between.

He Lives

It's been years since
my disgusting suitor
stopped calling.
He used to invade my dreams,
sometimes holding my hand,
pouring his meanness into me.

He had an impeccable
black suit,
impeccable
white hands
& four eyes.
Yesterday a friend said
"I dreamt I was in a fire
& a few yards away
a four-eyed man
was watching me."

I know him, I said.
I know him, I said.
I know him, I said.
He is dreadful.

Hey, who are you, Four-eyes?
Here I come, falling asleep.

Lina's Eyes

Lina, my blind colleague,
always came to classes
with her mother.
They'd take the front seats
& while her mother jotted notes
Lina listened with a solemn face.
(I heard it was a medical mistake —
the nurse pushed the wrong button,
the technicians did not repair the laser?)
Once I dared meet her gaze,
peeped out of my eyes
& waved a signal lamp as
they do directing aeroplanes.
I saw just two blank windows.
Behind the masonry a prisoner
walked to & fro hoping to get
used to the darkness.

Mirrors

I

Every night I look for a door to your dream.
I will open it & eavesdrop.
Although I have opened many doors
behind each one
I saw a mirror.

II

Do you remember how once we posed
naked & smiling before the mirror?
You and he swapped wives
& each kissed the other —
dreaming of oneself.

III

One day I will run through the mirror
as though through an old album.
Maybe I will find
unexpected pictures.
Yet I will miss one thing — the familiar
face before me.

IV

Mirror-people have no memory —
they look into your eyes & say:
I am the one from yesterday.
I am the one from the day before yesterday.
No, I tell them,
I am the one from yesterday
& you don't even know each other.

V

Maybe out of boredom
I looked around,
saw you,
smiled,
stretched out my hand.
You stretched your hand,
smiled —
you saw me,
looked around,
maybe out of boredom.

VI

My room has a window
looking outside
& a mirror looking inside.
At the window I meet the daylight.
At night I walk inside the mirror.

The School

was waiting
for the children, doors gaping.
The teacher in charge offered
a mumbled greeting.
Behind the flowers nobody
dared smile.
The barred panes stalked them,
muzzle-eyed.

In raggle-taggle order
 — owing to lack of practice —
& without singing
(everybody knew
a different song)
the children were led by twos
towards the entrance:
little black notes
from a marching tune
sung outside in.

To you, Wherever You Are

A bit of news I knew
but did not want to hear.
Where did this screen between you
& my memory come from?
We have been trying to end
an impossible game of chess:
you with black pieces on black squares,
I with white figures on white.
There was a joke I never
got to tell you — I am still
repeating it to myself.
Everything began with the dummy
we buried under your name.
It was only you who did not come to see.

O

The dog running at my heels
to guard me against the others
& snarl at me in private
carries my soul.
I am the soul's image
running round the tower
with the dog.
We are the hands of a clock —
the tower is a centre
& traces of our feet are
the only symbols on the clock-face.
These symbols — incomprehensible to us.
We just put them down.

Did time run out?
  Did time run
    out? Did
     time
     run
      out?

Mythologies

THESEUS

Was it his breathing or only wind
rushing along the corridors?

Theseus aimed a blow
& his sword rang against another.

Sparks flew.

Theseus saw the Minotaur
& could not understand the gods.
The Minotaur saw Theseus
& gaped in astonishment
"What? You've come to fight me
while a woman is pulling your string?"

— & burst out in laughter.
Theseus halved him as he was laughing.

PERSEPHONE

Mama,
stop chasing me.
Here in darkness I already know
I won't let you tuck me
back in your belly.
True, I hate him — he's involved
in terrible things —
but I ate the pomegranate
&, you know, I liked it.
Please,

please,
let me go.
I have to fulfil my own fears.

PERSEUS

"Who warned you to look at my reflection in the shield?"
"Athene"
"Who put the sickle that is not for reaping in your hand?"
"Hermes"
"Who did you take the magic helmet from?"
"Hades"
"I see you have powerful friends."

"Well, I reckon that's right. Anyway, prepare because
I'm about to chop your head off. The earth is no place for
monsters like you. Everybody says so, & I'm sure to become
a hero. "Perseus" the fortune-teller said "mark my words,
you will become a hero — now drop two gold pieces in the
cauldron & see if they'll disappear." Guess what, they
disappeared! The future belongs to heroes."

"Then come on, son,
do what you've come for
so I won't have to look
at your stupid face anymore."

After this Imperceptible Calm

Darling, unbind me from this bed,
take off the rings,
change the bandages.

What happened to me
the strongest among axe-throwers?

An old Mesopotamian Legend about Gilgamesh, King of Uruk, who wanted to become Immortal

Wanted to;
could not.

A Solemn Trip to the Family Roots

The mountains
of my grandfather's village
hate me.
Inhale me suspiciously
like a teenage first-time smoker.
The village,
a fungus growing on the hillside,
watches through squinting windows.
I visit a famous cave —
small gesture of politeness
towards the local sights —

water-mills thunder in its intestines.
The earth is alive.

I try not to leave any traces.

Auntie

Here comes my father's sister.
I can barely see her in her garden
among lush chrysanthemums,
hysterically wanton dahlias,
nodding yellow flower-clusters
too thin-necked to bear their beauty.

My aunt is a small woman
half-hidden under a scarf.
She walks slowly like a black bug.
Her noiseless shadow
follows among the flower stalks.

She has been twice married —
I can scarcely believe it.
The past has been devoured
by her tumbledown little house
& ivy widening the cracks.
Yet her faded face says nothing —
just exists among the chrysanthemums
& feeds them.

Those chrysanthemums look
as though grown in a slaughterhouse.

A Moment Before Perfection

Yully, the talk & vodka
are not bad because we know
we can always
start a new life — although,
if you ask me, I cannot say
what is wrong with this one.

A Lament for the Saintly Mothers

I hate poets who go into raptures
because their mothers have turned
into worn-out madonnas.
Drudgery at home, drudgery in the fields,
& a rhyming son comes home,
drinks with friends,
gets a clean shirt
(in case, around the corner,
he meets death;
or possibly
someone better-looking)
& then he goes out again, heart full of pity
for his mother's sorry look.
People who have turned
their mothers into saints
have no excuse.

At least I do not see any.

Sofia

Uneven lines of lamps —
some bright, others smashed.
Silent wake
of a Mercedes
sweeps across my face,
cigarette smoke
of a bully.
Asphalt mimics the sky
for colour and firmness.
The bingo hall is open,
the church is under repairs,
Coca-Cola wishes us
Merry Christmas.
In my empty pockets
I keep my fingers crossed
for the oboist
with his hat at his feet.

Freight Depot

...it explains why
there are no quays in Sofia
or streets free
of bits of beer bottles.

A boy & girl are walking hand in hand
talking about an episode on TV.
She walks in her slippers
between the housing blocks;
he seems readier
for life — his sneakers
have started sneaking.
They look engaged — here people
get engaged first.
One day old folks will gather,
give them a couple
of blankets & new linen
& a chicken
will die in the pot
without having ever
stepped out of the cage.

First Blood

Mutilated doll by the garbage bin —
looked like practice
            for something
bigger.

According to a Specialist's Opinion

You are watching
a football match.
I am making salad
just for myself.
I know already
to be lonely is when
you are with somebody
who is not with you.

Fused

First time I saw you
I kissed my inner man goodbye
& he just smiled
"Did you recognize him?"
he whispered in my ear.
Slowly he stepped out
& stood beside you
like something from an adventure novel.
Though his lion's mane
was lighter than your hair,
though he was smiling
like a kid who'd just shot the neighbour's cat,
someone focused the picture
& you fused with each other.
You swallowed him with the power
of truth that can be touched.

Yet sometimes
I see you toss your lion's head
& burst into laughter
like a kid who's just shot the neighbour's cat.
I throw a kiss at the rascal
who left me
on the day we met.

Morning

comes out of the blue
with free freshness
& a babble of dying stars.
The stairwell smells of coffee.
Behind doors
people are weightless.
At bus stops they nestle
against invisible pillows
& hope to hear someone's voice announce

False start.
Morning is cancelled.
Back to bed, all of you.

I am a Bad Warder

The bird is whistling
& clearly
does not mind the cage bars.

They have always been there.

I give him as much
food as I want
to be given myself.

Every day I feel like setting him free.

Yet I never do — freedom,
for him, would be lethal.
I already know

I am one of those weak people

who would never by the bed
of someone
suffering from cancer
offer poison.

Accident

As if a hawk's wing slashed my neck.
"You'd better not look."
Behind my eyelids I see spots;
outside them, I trace the outlines of….
"You'd better not look."
Clean up. Turn the world into what it was
before I closed my eyes.
"Then —
you'd better not look."

In the Train

In the train
an old Hungarian
woman without
front teeth
told me that two
of her three children
had died
& her oldest son

is now in America —
these are the photos,
there he is,
this is his family.
She smoked Bulgarian
cigarettes or rather
one very long
cigarette from Budapest

to Bucharest
& she said
"Now I have
nothing to live for".
said it simply,
plainly, flatly,
with the dignity
of the toothless.

Dry Needle

A little man once told me
"I made a robot that pierces people
& they drip out."

He showed it to me
— it was true.
Then he added thoughtfully

"We all live our own lives;
me, you, everyone."
"What has this got to do with the robot?"

"A lot, a great lot."

Half-turns

When the suicide
flew past my window
I was drinking coffee & milk —
very thin, for my nerves.
When the man
flew by
my watch showed ten to six
& thirty eight seconds...
perhaps he flew until the fortieth;
I cannot say for sure,
cannot say when
exactly the seconds
became insignificant.
My whole day turned
upsidedown,
I threw up the coffee,
but the gesture was devoid
of magical significance.

Poem about the Father who ate his Watches

On his left hand he wore
three watches.
"Why do you need all three?"

"This one" he said — pointing to the first
"shows what time it will be
in half an hour."

"This one" — pointing to the second
"shows what time it was
half an hour ago."

"As for this one" — pointing to the third
"it shows what the time is
now."

"All right, would you now give me the exact time?"
"Ha-ha, don't worry
it will come."

Over each Head Hangs a Star on a Thread

Among the cars
the gypsyman's cart
crawls.

His moustache tobacco-yellowed,
his grandson perched on a separate plank;
busiest of all, the little donkey with the tassels:
three heads, equally unkempt.

The man next to me hides behind a newspaper,
a woman asks me about bus times;
I pass by because
I do not know the exact answers
& anyway I try to keep away
from people with pedantic diction.

I see the vanishing
thin back of the child
& we all disappear
on separate planks.

A Face under the Ice

I need to remember.
I must remember.
Yet I cannot.
Something is
stopping me... the face
is unknown.
A face is in the way — a screen
hides a figure & I cannot
peep through.
How can I see him
behind the screen:
he might be
ill & waiting, or scarred
& in need of a face.
Now he is
lost in my memory.
Falling
I break, back first,
through strata.
The holes keep my form
but have no meaning.
There is nothing I can clutch.
Still puzzled
I pass by.

The Night when the Earth was Infested by Fufilled Wishes

Now I feel easy
because I expect nothing.
The roughly polished glass
of the North Sea
is far off, yet through
a roundabout way
reaching the equator.
Africa (blue nomads
among man-eating sands)
a week ago
lent its back to a Leonid shower:
stars fell
piercing through hot & cold
atmospheric layers
& people in countries
with unclouded skies
made wishes.
The papers say that in China
a falling star killed a man.
I think I know
what he wished.
It is possible.

The Wall by the Swings

The children swing to unearthly music,
three pendulums measuring different times.
Somebody has scratched on the house wall

I will be back for you

in needlessly deep letters.

Every Picture Can Stand Numberless Shakings

In the difficult part of the picture
I saw my own future, undistinguishable
from problems clutching my body —

I needed a new perspective

so I shook the picture
& saw an old man turned into a boy
scattering shiny dust over the universe;
from the dust, flowers, new stars cropped
to snow on the earth where necessary
& by him stood a red-haired woman,
an infinite
infinite woman laughing
& then I knew
I could be either of the two.

9.55, 5 Minutes before the Beginning

The executioner took off his mask.
The prisoner took off his hood.
They had identical faces.
One told the other:
this is strange but it does
not change a thing.
It's not even important.
The problem now
is how to kill
the infinite five minutes.

The Master of Silence

The master of silence
painted a root.
The root unfolded into a tree.
It invaded the sky
like a moist watercolour
changing the season with its hues.
The wind spread a rumour
of transparent fruit.
The master of silence
looked at it, looked again, then finally,
regretting his own lack of talent,
crumpled the leaf.

Scent of Afternoon Resin

When for the first time
I rubbed cypress cones
into my palm
somebody said
"Summer is almost over."

I don't like summer
but the matter, so put,
saddens me.

In the Streetcar

Standing upright
I grip the bar
of the seat in front of me
with both hands.
In the seat an old woman trembles.
It seems as if I am pushing
the wheelchair of a disabled person.
I'll push until she gets off
& then I'll somersault
into the seat,
grey-haired.

Outside the world always
looks new.

I Am Somebody Else's Thought

As my pen nears the paper
I hear a hush.
I touch the page lightly

& a whisper comes
"Now she will write..."
I cannot hear.

"She will pull,
pull, pull coiling
through the eye of the nib the thread

to which we are connected."
— "I pull nothing."
— "Through which we live

in the world behind."
— "The world beyond."
— "No, the world behind

& through these scribbles
we pass to the front world."
I said:

"We don't have clear outlines
so we take them from you."
I read:

"We have no end
so we make use
of yours."

The Local School

The first thing one can see over the heads
of the sturdy guys in sleeveless undershirts
chasing the neighbourhood football
are the portraits of big-time national writers
on the blind wall of the school.
Their eyes are painted so as to stare
into the future;
I suspect they secretly
watch the match;
their faces, somewhat reproachfully,
take the crooked passes as a chance
of limited participation.
THE HEADMASTER IS A NAZY
is written near the main entrance
& **HOUSE OF PAIN**
under the portraits —
no spelling mistakes this time.
Someone has taken
his literacy from here,
used it to express himself —
as far as he could,
as best he could,
as far as he has taken it,
far as he was given — an ink suit
for a wedding day, for a funeral,
or rather
a sleeveless undershirt.

A Life-long Invitation

What do you think about the posters?

Oh, the posters?
They are wall plugs
whose cables
lead to events —
inviting me to attend,
sucking me in.

Sucking you in?

They are appealing somehow.

Appealing?

Oh, the posters.
They are not for me. Somebody
is hiding the walls with them.

Beliefs

Old people say that whenever
someone lights a cigarette from a candle
a sailor dies.

Among sailors, I suppose,
there is a belief that when they shave
in an odd direction, an academic dies.

So they try not to shave.
The point is that we think
about each other.

Our Plans

She washed the meat in the plates,
wiped the webs from her face,
stitched up the beds,
watered the oven,
stewed the telephone with butter
& put a pillow over each lamp
to make their place really cozy.
"Meanwhile," she said,
"all thoughts about our plans
are postponed."

The Snake

slowly crept
up my knees.
"Ha, Ha!" Freudians would interpose,
"we all know
what kind of snake that is."
"No," is the right answer,
"This is another snake."

The Loving Husband

In his inside compartment he always carried
her image — a human-shaped beaker
filled with a velvet
organic solution & spare eyes.

She was, in reality, an obscure
person with definite needs.

He died in love with his wife.
She lived unloved.

Essay: If all Professions were Available which one would you choose

I want to be a prince
not a princess — not an object
of socially dynamic passions,
family contracts
or nation-wide moustache twisting.
No. It is not cool to be an object
but something more subjective —
a prince for instance,
nodding absent-mindedly: Oh, yes
                              Oh, no
gazing into *Magnolia grandiflora* on his lapel —
heavy with protocol knowledge,
light on the heavier stuff.
Enough for the world the way he is,
neither beautiful
nor intelligent:
a zero behind
which all other numbers align —
surrounded by animate & inanimate matter
invisible even
after the thought
"all this will be mine" —
like a birthmark
the face has grown used to —
in the middle of all commotion
free of himself.

Your Father Now

is far away,
he is old & picking lilies
in a infinite field —
after each cut flower
apologizing "I didn't know,
I didn't know
this too might hurt."
No, he is not picking lilies
but poppies
& they trickle down his fingers.

Pet Nurse

She came in with fresh meat.

The young eagle
had already
grown heavy
talons, beak
feathering off
the last fluffy tufts.
"Oh, look at yourself"
said the woman. "I worried
whether you'd live!"
He turned his new eye
towards her
& this time
did not notice her.

All Power to the Hands of the Anarchists

"Art is in the streets of Stockholm" said Johan
which meant
"I'm sorry about the boring private art galleries".
He apologized for the rain also
although I didn't mind it at all.

> *"I don't smoke*
> *I don't drink*
> *I don't fuck*
> *at least I can fuckin' think"* Johan roared
> along with his favourite punk band.
> His hair, the crest of a blond Mohican,
> was fastened with a rubber band.

"Oh, give me a break!"

> "OK" he gave in. "I don't live
> up to my principles
>
> sometimes I get drunk."

When the time comes to pull down the world order
Johan will be pulling from Stockholm & I from Sofia.
That's what I've promised. Meanwhile

> art is in the streets of Stockholm.
> Johan hangs around unemployed.

About the Fire

The pair try to light a fire.
Surrounding silence coughs
through the leaves' redness.

The first one is tall,
with a widow's peak.
The second was in love some time ago

but has stopped talking about it.
The two are all alone
both separately & together.

Only the fire
unites them
& it will not light.

Warned by leafy rustling,
they cup the sticks,
add paper, wait

for the new air to settle,
then strike matches.
But not too near

because in order
to stay together
they must not succeed.

I add this sheet of paper.

Illumael

*

"What's your name?"
I asked him "I think
I know you but don't know
your name."
"Just say a name
& it will be mine."
"You mean I'll
give you a name?"
"No, you'll only
guess it right."
"Illumael!"

**

"Illumael, is there
anything I can do for you?"
"Do something good for others
& it will come to me."
"So whatever I do
I should say *It's for him*?"
"No, I have no third person
being only I
or you."

***

Once again we were
talking together.
"Illumael
you haven't got wings but
they might look good on you."
Illumael said
"We have no wings
because we cannot
help flying,"

In the Park

From another world
this wind, weird.
First warm, then cold.
Half-heartedly foreknowing springtime.
Gluing women's locks over rouged lips.
Blowing out lighters carried to faces.
Throwing dust in the eyes.
Mooring people to benches.
Lovers forgot to show off before each other
& dazedly looked ahead.
Embracing. Unblinking.
Each of them having run
for a moment to old friends.

Summing-up

Santa Claus
you have given me a broken toy!
That's OK, son — what matters
is that you have been a good boy.

A Visit to the Clockmaker

I crossed the street
to enter a secret shop
where hundreds of hands grind time.

Charted small faces leave aside their arguments
about missing moments & start
ticking reproachfully, peep
out of three walls of shelves.
Two alarm clocks
ponderously hurdle the minutes.
A grandfather clock with a pendulum necktie
shows me the way.
A sunbeam
inscribes on the counter
its own vision of accuracy.
Down there, the clockmaker
is tinkering with the open intestines
of a disbatteried body.

His door rang its bell.

"A new timepiece?"
I dislike giving false hope
so I said "A new chain, please."

Then thought *One who will manage to slice*
time into amazingly thin straps
& thus make good use of his life
will be the happiest of us all.

The clockmaker raised his gaze
& would not agree.